POETICALLY BLACK

REFLECTIONS ON AFRICAN AMERICAN
JOY, SORROW, AND HEALING

poems

JANIS LESLIE EVANS

JAHMERICAN PRESS

Jahmerican Press

www.janislevans.com

For permissions and special orders, contact: evanscounseling@jlevanslpc.com.

POETICALLY BLACK: REFLECTIONS ON AFRICAN AMERICAN JOY, SORROW, AND HEALING

Copyright ©2023 by Janis Leslie Evans

Cover art © Janis Leslie Evans

Cover design & Interior typesetting by Vanessa Anderson at NightOwlFreelance.com

Printed in the United States
Paperback ISBN-13: 978-1-949193-37-4

"We write because we believe the human spirit cannot be tamed and should not be silenced."

~ *Nikki Giovanni*

CONTENTS

CONTENTS

A POETIC DEDICATION TO THE CULTURE

"Poetry is language at its most distilled and most powerful."
~ *Rita Dove*

Poetry for me has been a creative expression of emotions and words that start in my head and churn in my soul. I simply refer to it as a creative play on words. When verse forms are applied to those words, my poetry gets its structure, rhythm, and appeal. However, form and structure alone does not the perfect poem make. Of course, there is no such thing as perfection in such a subjective art form as poetry, except, of course, that which is found in the eye of the beholder. But the one sure thing about writing poetry is that it is a sacred process out of which poets, spoken word artists, and rappers alike share from the deepest and most intimate places of their souls. That process is what makes the act of writing poetry and rhyme an extraordinary vehicle, whereby the gift of powerful expression is created and shared with others and archived into eternity. In my poem, "Word Play," written in 2013, I share the sacredness of this process, using no specific structure or verse form. It could very well be categorized as inspirational poetry.

I dedicate this poem and book to those poets who share their poetry in the African American tradition of storytelling. I honor poet ancestors like Maya Angelou, Langston Hughes, and Gwendolyn Brooks, who brought to life the stories of our rich history and layered experiences with joy, pain, sorrow, celebration, and healing. I celebrate professors like Nikki Giovanni and activists like Kevin Powell who carry on the storytelling of our culture today in poetic form. I humbly join you as I present my second book, a collection of poems, an extension of the recollections I shared in my first book.

Word Play

Quiet expression in word form
Bursts in living color
No need to say it loudly
The words speak for themselves

Flowing in from dark places
Illustrated by arrangements
So original in their display
None of which are the same

The light of my keystroke
Ignites one letter at a time
Creating each word play
As verses are formed

Spirited words generate
Moving from pen to paper
Uncontrolled in the moment
A surge begins to gel

Verses come alive with meaning
Expressions of thought and feeling
Infinitely depicts experiences
In descriptive word play

I wait to see what comes
In the form it takes
Naturally, without a plan
Each word born out of seed

Seeds planted from lessons
Things seen and heard
Encounters to pull from
People I've met along the way

Life is rich with this soil
Out of which I grow
And capture in verse
Immortalizing word play

Sharing with others in echoes
Bouncing from present to future
Through open eyes and ears
Received by hearts and souls

"Poetry is the lifeblood of rebellion, revolution, and the raising of consciousness."

~ *Alice Walker*

PART I

HOW THEY SEE US

Clouded Perceptions of Black Men

I look your way, not to harm
I envy your position in life

I stare at your property, not to steal
But to imagine if only I could afford the gift

My feet drag, not because I'm shiftless
I tire from working two shifts

My face appears hard, not from criminality
I'm angry because I just got laid off

I dress like this, not for lack of self-respect
It's the best I can do for now

I would love to have disposable income
But there isn't much left after expenses

So when you see me through your clouds
Stop to adjust your view

What you think you see may not be my true self
So let up and relax your critical nature

Reach out to me non-judgmentally
Greet me with a nod, not a scowl

Do not fear but pray for me, and you,
for all your stereotypes of me, will be extracted

Leaving your mind open to see clearly
Our real humanity beneath the skin

Black Friends

We are the chosen ones,
The token and the blessed,
The very lucky few,
Much better than the rest.

We are educated,
We sound as if we're white,
Articulating perfectly,
Our diction is just right.

They love to say about us,
"You are not like them,"
Boasting of the friendships
"Those are my good Black friends."

They have no clue indeed,
The insult that we feel,
Referring to our people,
As if they were not real.

"YES, I have some Black friends,"
They say aloud with pride,
While statements made in secret,
Reveal another side.

What "privilege" we have earned!
To be such *good* Black friends,

Upholding token status,
Until convenience ends.

The Elevator Door Closed

I entered the car while they stayed behind,
I waited. And I waited.
And waited, holding the door,
Like a Pullman porter for the family of three.

They looked away and the elevator door closed.
I wondered. And I wondered.
And wondered, as the car ascended.

Did my smile turn them off,
Or was it my puffy purple parka and fuzzy red cowl,
Or my black coarse hair and dark brown skin,
Making friendly eye contact impossible?

The car ascended, rising above pettiness
Passing all floors of bigotry and fear,
Leaving a racist act of ignorance on the lower level
Where it belongs.

Survival Instincts

Images of death etched in place
So many rolling like films
Running on auto-play
They know how these movies end

The plots are the same
Black men and boys
Afraid to die in vain
Dying to stay alive
The goal is to escape death
Survive the confrontation
Avoid becoming the next image
In the minds of the next

Fight or flight instincts at work
Survival of the fittest
History's past and present says
Run for your life, don't trust

"Why didn't you stop?"
"Why did you run?"
"Why don't you comply?"
"Why, why, why?"

"Put your hands up!"
"Don't move!"
"Let me see your hands!"

"Don't move!"

"Get down on the ground!"
"Simon says, don't move!"
"Let me see your license!"
"I didn't say Simon says!"

"Shots fired, shots fired!"
"Momma, momma!"
"Man down, man down!"
"I told him not to move."

Black men and boys
Programmed by human nature
To avoid death at all costs
Driven by survival instincts

Black Woman's Burden

The world's weight was hers
Sailing from one shore to another
To care for hers and theirs
Able bosom and strong hips
Nurse and hold the babes

Her nurturing genes are innate
Poured into her from generations
Representing Kings and Queens
To serve hers and theirs
Infinite strength of motherhood

High expectations precede her
Caretaker of all things
Multi-tasker extraordinaire
To take on hers and theirs
With no complaints

Imprints of responsibility
Passed down through blood
Heavy lifting comes naturally
To carry hers and theirs
From here to eternity

A vessel to store emotion
A conduit of love to give
Storing life's pain

Holding hers and theirs
Her capacity has no limit

The strength of Black women
Celebrated every day
We look to her for care
To carry hers and theirs
Despite her heavy burden

The Deli

Slicing up your lunchmeat,
Waiting hand and knee
Always at your service
I tend to every need

Serving as your token Black
the first in history,
With apron tied and hairnet on
"Can I help you, please?"

How does one make history
In 1981
There is a first for everything
Our work is never done

Some of you look at me in awe
With horror and surprise
"A Black girl in the deli?"
Oh me, oh my, you sigh

I work inside your deli, yes!
You stare and look at me
At your service with a smile
I'm graceful as can be

I study your behavior
As I slice your meat:

Smoked turkey, ham or knockwurst
Pastrami and roast beef

Little did your small minds know
As far as you can't see
I serve you up on part-time
And work on my degree

Some of you won't allow me
To touch your precious food
You'll wait for the white deli girl
My service you elude

I'll ask, "May I help you, ma'am?"
Knowing what you'll do
Pretending you don't hear me
I love to mess with you

One day I had to wait on you
Your half a pound sliced thin
The challenge of the century
I'm sure this time I'd win

But later on that evening,
A package was sent back
A half a pound bologna
Just because I'm Black

The lessons learned were hard to take
I took each one in stride
As the first Black deli girl,
I sliced lunchmeat with pride

"We wear the mask that grins and lies, it hides our cheeks and shades our eyes."
~ *Paul Laurence Dunbar*

PART II

SELF-IMAGE/SKIN COLOR

Dirty Skin

Out of his ignorant eye, he saw my "dirty skin"
Into my innocent ear I heard, but was perplexed.

He repeated in his Canadian-Anglo tone
"Ur skinz durtee!"

Confused as I couldn't find the soil,
He smiled sardonically as he laughed,
Looking, for the first time, at a black child.

Like the bruised apple of the bunch,
Or the over-ripe brown banana in the fruit bowl
I was damaged goods in the eye of a little White boy

For the first time, I understood anger and shame.
Around age nine, for the first time,
I felt insulted.

Then I knew, for the first time,
What it means as a little Black girl
To have "dirty" skin.

Untamable

I won't behave today
You are too fickle
You manipulate me daily
I can't take the heat!
Expecting me to be flexible
To bend, lay, coil, and stay
The way you want me to
I'm tired of being stretched
Depending on your whim
Or weather forecast
Make up your mind, sis!
Stop tugging on me
I can't please you every day
Just let me, be me, naturally
Free me to do what I do
Let me have a good hair day
Naturally

Infinite Textures

Our hair presents so varied
Many grades of textures in form
Like rainbows of infinite color
Bleeding from hot to lukewarm

Bombarded with new products
Our coarse hair cannot use
Promises pop on Instagram
By the social-media muse

My fuzzy hair won't do that!
I shout at the iPhone screen
4c-coil to be tamed by
Creams and oils touted supreme

Don't you see, the hair we wear
Each crown sits high, alone
Unique as shades of skin tone
Embracing a texture all its own

Wavy or nappy, soft to touch
Versatility, the new brand
Cornrows, braids, or locks
Where does my type4 land?

Black hair made genetically
Comes by kinfolk blood

Tighter coils mean blacker juice
Create hues like beach sand or mud

How to care for our black hair
Varied as seashells and snowflakes
Waiting for that magic potion
What a fuss our hair makes

Double-Consciousness

Confidence of a lioness' roar
Hides the purrs of a scared kitten
Expecting evaluations of my skin
Criticism of my colorfully adorned body
And intrigue about my articulation.

I know my worth
But second guess myself
Re-calculating my value at every turn
While my ever-changing hairstyles
Trigger perplexed stares and questions.

I maintain cultural authenticity
While I straddle adherence to expectations
In constant conversations in my head,
Bouncing from one topic to the next
Hearing the slights, exchanging pleasantries,

Making the best impression outwardly
While seething with anger inside,
Trying to make sense of the micro-aggression
Unintended yet so piercing to the soul
Dodging subtle insults to ensure approval.

Internal dialogue is the norm
Black psyche true to form
Into this life we are born,

In perpetual state of White scorn
ONE SELF into two, is torn.

Self-Preservation

We hide behind our veils
Protected from eyes with closed minds
Meanings distorted by merged hues
Blurred by a false sense of self
Shadows created by lies and half-truths

Covered by perfunctory gestures
Accepting that which is familiar
We lose sight of who we are
Shielded by intentional denial
We feign ignorance

Like heavy venetian blinds
Offering little to no transparency
Letting in the desired amount of light
Controlling who we allow inside
While dimming our own shine

Feeling safer behind the scenes
Afraid of who we weren't meant to be
We pass each other in shadow form
Avoiding the true reveal
With no risk of rejection

Slight glimpses of us trail away
Drifting into the ethers of escape
Crying out to be hidden no more

Hesitant to shed our masks
We remain our shadow selves

"Poetry is a political act because
it involves telling the truth."
~ *June Jordan*

PART III

PERSECUTION AND MENTAL WELL-BEING

Somebody's Watchin' Me

Like a city monument, people look at me
As if I'm public property in Washington, DC

Who they think they lookin' at with their
intrusive beady eyes
I walk the streets uncomfortably; they stare and pass me by

I know I am on display, though I tell myself I'm not
Gazers know in this side show, I'm character and plot

The center of attraction, everywhere I go
Pointed fingers, piercing eyes, anticipate the show

They talk about me endlessly, defenseless as I am
They judge me from the outside in, not as I really am

Like damaged goods, they pick out fault,
as if that's all they see
And if they could, I'm sure they would take my last from me

Unlike a city monument or public property
I wish I could reclaim myself and all my dignity

Fear of Exposure

An unexpected meeting place, by choice or circumstance
Opening myself to you in a therapeutic stance

Who is this, I ask myself, a stranger in my face
Expecting me to give details and share with you my case

Crazy disposition laid, to open up and talk
While you just sit still listening and watch me like a hawk

More and more I talk about the things that make me shrink
Feeling very vulnerable, I wonder what you think

As time passes on the clock, with so much more to say
A tug-of-war I play inside, true feelings held at bay

I don't think I can trust this thing, the dance called therapy
Exposed and naked there I sit as you look back at me

Your judgment and analysis slowly brings forth my fears
Afraid to show you all of me as I hold back my tears

I cannot trust you entirely, my affect fades to blank
I retreat inside my head back to my cold think tank

For now, I will protect myself with every chosen word
Sharing with you only from the tip of my iceberg

Insurrection

Predominantly White men representing
Their kinfolk, moving as one
Like a disruptive hailstorm
Wrecking a small town

My eyes held captive by the scene
Surreal violence escalating like a tsunami
As men morphed into wild animals
Released from their cages of democracy

They scaled walls, broke windows
Crashed down doors, breached barriers
Pillaged sacred ground with glee
Having no regard or conscience

Sorrow and anger filled my soul
Dismay and fear grew within
Fueled by disbelief
My Black skin shivered

Stress-based reactions of a siege
Implode and seethe inside me
As White men destroy with purpose
On a mission to covet the country

Their boldness shook me
As they attacked the guardians

Sworn to protect them and us
With their warped sense of justice

The images evoked terror
Displays of arrogance and privilege
Worse than the violence itself
As they took over the People's house

Chaos filled the solemn halls
Reserved for civil discourse
The air rang with threats of violence
Echoes still heard by the victims

My rage heightened to new levels
I watched this for hours
Pondering my safety into the night
Will they move into neighborhoods?

Who will stop them?
The insane power of White supremacy
Hell bent on ruthless occupation
Left me sick and afraid in my Black skin

Triggers

Rainy day
Cloudy gray
Get up, you say?
In bed, I'll stay
If I may
In warmth, I lay
Please, go away
Don't want to play

Buried here
Can't comb my hair
Nothing to wear
In despair
Won't go nowhere
At walls, I stare
Life's unfair
Too much to bear
No love to share

Never Enough

Roses are red
Skies are blue
I still need to prove it to you

Water is wet
Clear as day
You don't believe a word I say

Fire is hot
Burns the skin
From your perspective, I can't win

The Earth is round
On axis it turns
You say there is your history to learn

Ice is cold
Freezing to touch
Your denial is becoming too much

I took life's test
A passing grade
You won't accept the progress I've made

I've proven my worth
You will not see
Beyond your biased perception of me

Conversations with White People

If I seem distracted, it's not you
I'm feeling split in two
It's just racial trauma

If I act defensive, nothing personal
I'm feeling protective
It's my racial trauma

If I seem jumpy, I won't hit you,
It's just that your skin is a trigger
That's racial trauma

When I get agitated listening to you
I'm reminded of a racist I once knew
The manifestation of racial trauma

If my attention trails, no worries
I hear you loud and clear
You triggered my racial trauma

If I forget what you said, pardon me
I'm listening to the conversation in my head
Caused by racial trauma

If I look away, no disrespect
Just taking a deep breath
To cope with racial trauma

"We are each other's harvest; we are each other's business; we are each other's magnitude and burden."
~ *Gwendolyn Brooks*

PART IV

FAMILY/COMMUNITY/RELATIONAL DYNAMICS

The Spirit of Black Motherhood

That tragic hour, cut to her core
Jagged edge of violence severed the bond
Between mother and child
A painful rend in heart, mind and soul

Is such a wound repairable?
A daily occurrence in a community
Filled with collective sorrow
Virtuous characters of women survive

A mother's love never ends, transcending loss
Beyond the destruction caused by bullets
Rising above and beyond the catastrophe of sudden death
The turning point at which grief eases with time

Motherhood spirit rises out of the dust
Black-momma love overcomes darkness and pain
She continues to give from her broken heart
To heal her community

Wounds patched by God's love
Received through her child
Hollow spaces filled by acts of kindness
Her child's memory honored by service

Blessed at her expense and sacrifice
She leads us in the march

Unselfishly becoming the change
Doing what comes naturally

Her strength rooted in faith and love
Overcomes challenges of loss and tragedy
A phoenix rising to the occasion
Touching the lives of others to remember her child

Only In My Dreams

I see you rarely, late at night
Memories come and go
I miss you, brother, in my dreams
Like the first coating of snow

Imagining protecting you
Safe from all life's harms
As I grab your little hand
I hold you in my arms

I see you singing in the choir
Your beautiful tenor sound
I long to hear your voice again
Your pitch and tone abound

I lost you, oh so tragically
An early death you met
My dear sweet baby brother's gone
I can't let go, not yet

I look to see you nightly still
I wish you'd come to me
As I lay down inside my head
Your face I wait to see

A Cry for Momma

Abandoned like a baby in a crib
I cry for momma

You leave me for hours alone
To peer through crib bars in tears

I need to be fed daily
I'm starving for your love

When will you hold me
I long for your touch

Where did you go
Are you coming back

You promised to always be there
I wait for your return

How can I trust you
To come when I call

I will never love again
As I cry out for momma

When Will We Overcome

Each win brings another challenge
When we thought it was over
Our last fight until the end
One more battle to transcend

Mental bondage of the weary
Invisible chains of oppression
Sealed in place by systemic glue
Will we overcome, I ask you

Generations of pain passed on
One family's trauma to the next
Unspoken but seen in faces contorted
Hope-filled souls with dreams thwarted

Good fights expressed in protest and riot
Demanding equality, justice, and peace
Re-emerge in eras as events repeat
Walking for miles rejecting defeat

Looking beyond what seems grim
Continuing struggles in new forms
Yet packaged in the same skin
Will we overcome, will we win

Ode to Karon Blake

Black boys runnin' wild
Looking for connection
Lost in space, out of place
Having no direction

Out here stealing cars
Easy hits they find
With one click, a lock they pick
Damage left behind

Pulled into the crew
Trying to belong
Then shot to death by resident
Tell me, who was wrong

Shocked in disbelief
Asking how and why
At thirteen, just a teen
How many more will die

Babies making money
Trapped by circumstance
Stealing cars for rides to Mars
No fear, they take a chance

Beloved community mourns
A family in grief

Trying to find the answer
Seeking justice and relief

Is it just the guns
Or layers of social ills
Or trigger-happy residents
Shooting kids at will

The wailing and the tears
Stretch far beyond DC
Black boys running rampant
Neighborhoods under siege

But in this solemn moment
I think of Karon Blake
A life with greater value
Than bullets and a car-break

Ode to Arianna Davis

Riding in the back seat
tucked safely in with family
on Mother's Day

Flying bullets heard
Pierces car and innocence
upper body wounds

Hail of bullets rend a family's
Celebration Sunday broken.
Forever. Broken.

Car rides used to bring joy
Sunday packed in the back
headed to McDonald's

Sundays were safe and fun
After church, after groceries
hamburger and fries

Rode trips, rides to Haines Point
Games in the back seat
counting Volkswagens

No barrage of bullets
Interrupting peace
assaulting blue skies

What in the actual . . uck!
Are 10-year-olds doing
riding safely with family—
and dying—anyway?!?

Blessed angel ripped away
Safe now in the arms of Christ.
Left a void. On Mother's Day.

"When you are joyous, look deeper into your heart and you shall find it is only that which has given you sorrow that is giving you joy."
~ *Khalil Gibran, The Prophet*

PART V

HEALING WOUNDS AND FINDING PEACE

Burden Shift

Buried deep by circumstance
Nothing I can do
My life is suffocating me
I'll never make it through

Problems insurmountable
In tandem they do come
When I think the worst has passed
Here comes another one

I have left no stone unturned
I've gone through every maze
Exploring all alternatives
Passing through each phase

I've often thought of suicide
The easiest escape
Resorting to the cowardice
My own life I dare take

If only someone understood
The hurdles of my life
Help me move them one by one
Lessening my strife

Barely can I carry this
I soon will have to share

The truth about the tall brick walls
Life's traps are so unfair

I've mustered enough courage now
I ask you, "Please help me!
My burdens much too heavy
I pray you hear my plea

"Save me from my dark despair
Extract me from my grave
An early death I do not wish
A way out we will pave"

No longer must I sit alone
Nor carry the huge lift
My prayer made and answered
I feel life's burden shift

Mid-life Split

Caught between the pull of two
Both worlds encompass me
I straddle inside back and forth
To see who I should be

Commitments versus passion's call
To which do I adhere?
At the crossroads of my life
Confronted by my fears

Choices are in front of me
Which door do I pursue?
While obligations call me home
My heart has not a clue

Half my life has come and gone
With more still to be done
Time cannot be wasted when
Tomorrow may not come

I long for peace and happiness
Attained by very few
Pursuing passions put on hold
To mine own heart be true

Answers do elude me now
As I wait patiently

Consumed by indecisiveness
On love and loyalty

My common senses speak to me
They say, "You know what's right"
You have responsibilities
"WAKE UP, and see the light"

Realities are very clear
I know what I must do
Embrace the challenge of my life
Find balance in the two

Live each day as if it were
My last on God's green Earth
Accepting every blessing for
Its value and its worth

My choices come with drawbacks
They have their good points, too
I focus on my need for both
And change my point of view

I let go of conflicting thoughts
Releasing all control
My strength lies in a fresh approach
As new peace calms my soul

Each lesson will bring clarity
One crisis at a time
In the end, wisdom transcends
As I pass through my prime

Chasing Patience

Tests of will stretch us thin
Like used rubber bands, we give in
Our ability to hold on wanes with time
No more grip on life's steep climb

Who can attain an apex so high
Earth's lowly ones like you and me
We long for liberty to be free
From the long wait upon Thee

As we wait for "green lights"
Human impulse creates more plight
Tempers flare from zero to ten
Causing us to wait again

If only we could grasp the truth
Virtuous lessons learned in our youth
Waiting our turn will get us there
Then everyone else's chance is fair

Impatience stirs like strong wind
Blowing over our own kin
Forgetting to treat each other right
With only selfish needs in sight

If only we could stop and see
To be patient is the key

Since we are not in control
Of what we long for in our soul

Let it go with a little faith
No need for all the fervent haste
Things will happen when they will
So take a breath, wait . . . and be still

Loving Me

Despite thee
I love me
The way you see
Not good for me

I won't believe
How you see me
My love of me
Is the key

You don't perceive
My integrity
The real me
Like strong tea

Now leave me be
Away from me
Hear my decree
As I love me

Kuumba Chi

My chi, my chi, my Kuumba chi
Driven by God's love
Pushed forth by unique ancestral spirit
Circles within me

The raw, uninhibited flow of chi
Pours out of me
Without boundary

I see chi in all of we
Limitless movement inside
It grows, it weaves where it abides
Melding together as it takes form

The voice, the pen, the feet, the brush
The fingers, the hips shake
The word, the song, the dance, the frame
The spinning wheel creates

We present our Kuumba chi through our gifts
Individually wrapped as our own
Impossible to copy, infinite in kind
As we debut at show time

Our curtains draw back
Exposing the stage
We are not afraid

As Kuumba Chi makes its entrance
It puts smiles on faces, warms hearts,
And beautifies our community and world

My chi, my chi, my Kuumba chi
Letting me, be me
And we, be we

Reaching For Peace

As I look for calm within,
Distressing from the day
I reach for peace inside myself,
An exhale and a heartbeat away.

The peace that lives within my heart,
Is often hard to find,
Caught up inside life's chaos,
Stuck in my stressed-out mind.

To be centered is my goal,
Stability within,
Clearing out the daily noise,
Shutting out the din.

Praying, breathing, standing still,
I find my place of peace,
The pathway to my heart is clear,
Distractions will now cease.

Peace is just a breath away,
I get there at my will,
With God's help, I pause and say,
"Be calm, my heart, be still."

Like Water Flowing

Like water flowing, music moving at one speed,
Underneath the flow is a current of anxiety,
Rushing like waves, moving too fast.
But from the spectator, it flows freely at one pace,
As waist turns and limbs spread,
Rounded and extending to the tips of my fingers.
I push my hand through the air,
My body follows, and I take a gentle step,
Creating forms in sequences of full and empty.
My jing is good as it flows through the hands,
Everything moving in sync,
As I balance on one leg, shaking slightly.
I breathe to stay calm and steady,
As I try not to observe the observers,
And gracefully share with them my best tai chi.

On Perfection

nappy edges
let them be

imperfect world
look at me

natural hair
black cotton balls

touching the trees
at glorified heights

stomach puffy
not too flat

hips spread wide
curved silhouette

our own image
ancestors made proud

my perfect self
made beautifully

At the Age of Celebration

I celebrate today with . . .
no Color to hide my gray,
no Weaves
no Tracks
no Rinses

no Chemicals to straighten my hair,
no Wigs
no Pieces
no Extensions

no Flatteners to hold me in,
no Tucks
no Lifts
no Shapers

no Acrylics to extend my nails,
no Tips
no Tattoos
no Lashes

no Botox to puff my lips,
no Lipo
no Peels
no Injections

no Silicone to enlarge my breasts,

no Enhancements
no Reductions
no Plastics

no Fat to flavor my food,
no Salt
no Frying
no Excess

no Diets that I will fail,
no Pills
no Binges
no Starvation

no Smokes to light and inhale,
no Drugs
no Needles
no Addictions

no Cancer to take me out,
no Strokes
no Heart Attacks
no HIV

no Depression to take my joy,
no Guilt
no Self-Hatred
no Self-denial

In my prime, I celebrate naturally and joyfully,
counting my blessings and thanking my lucky stars.

Faces of Reunion

Our faces tell the stories
Expressions so unique
Brown, yellow, mocha, black, and tan
Our linkages we seek

So many stories to be told
Life's lessons we do share
Passed down from generations' past
The good and bad we bear

Aunties, uncles, cousins
Elders and brothers flock
Sisters, wives, and husbands, too
Solid as a rock

Linked by birth and blood and genes
Joined by marriage vows
Expanding our connections
Sometimes we don't know how

In any case we're family
Each one with tales to share
We ask and probe and get to know
The who, what, when, and where

Our faces tell the stories
Secrets of our pasts

In our eyes, the spirits live
From first kin to the last

Next Time, I'll Remember

Defined by their strengths
I carry on

Created in their image
I am royalty

Blooming daily like flowers
I shine in living color

Resting upon survival
I don't give up

Next time I complain
I'll remember

Those ancestors
who paved MY way

Those who endured
Pain and strife

For whom I honor
Like a bird in flight

Their last breath
under my wings

Forever lifted
Soaring to heights

Fulfilling their wildest dreams
of freedom and liberty

Like generations before me
I can't give in

I strive in elevation
of the ancestors

ACKNOWLEDGEMENTS

First, I must express honor and glory to God from where my blessings flow. Completing this project is a testament to my faith and a belief in a God who answers prayers. I am truly blessed to have been given the gift of writing as I fulfill His purpose for me on this Earth. I pray that my poetry touches the hearts and souls of those who need validation and healing from their racial trauma while celebrating the joys and triumphs of our African American culture.

I extend special thanks to Brenda Arledge, a fellow poet and writer at HubPages (The Arena Group), for igniting my creative juices over the last several years, to write more poetry. Some of these poems resulted from word prompt exercises she presents to our small community of poets on the writing site where we share, critique, and support each other's work. I am grateful to her and my fellow writers at HubPages for keeping me challenged. Thank you, Brenda, for being my muse.

Gratitude is extended to one of my favorite people, a poet and energy healer, Dr. Paula Potts. Her zeal as a multi-talented creator who has written two poetry books has contributed spiritually to my goal of producing my own book of poetry. Thank you, Paula, for your love, mentorship, and support.

I extend appreciation for another fellow poet and friend who I met on Facebook during her show on poetry and healing. We now refer to our destined connection as a sister-friendship. Thank you, Dr. Paulina Van, for your belief in my ability to touch people with my poetry in ways of which I was not fully aware and now embrace.

Finally, I am grateful to my husband Gregory, who provides steady patience as a spouse of a writer. He knows too well how I can get lost in time, writing for hours to the point of dinner time passing into delayed preparation and eating late. Thank you for your love and immeasurable support of my passion.

For readers who enjoyed my first book *Recollections About Race: Getting to the Roots and Healing,* thank you for wanting more.

ABOUT THE AUTHOR

Janis Leslie Evans, the "Healing Author," has been writing since she was a child. Born in Buffalo, New York, she is a first generation American born to Jamaican parents who immigrated from the Caribbean and Canada. Janis has been a resident of Washington, DC since 1982 when she entered Howard University as a graduate student and received her master's degree in counseling psychology. She received her bachelor's degree in psychology from State University of New York at Buffalo (now Buffalo State University). She is licensed to practice in the District of Columbia, is the sole owner of Evans Counseling & Consultation, PLLC, and provides individual and couples counseling, addressing relational conflicts, grief and loss, anxiety, depression, unresolved childhood trauma, and exposure to traumatic and life-altering events.

Janis has always loved writing poetry throughout her life and was first published at the age of 11 in an annual book published by Buffalo Public Schools, which highlighted the creative writing of its students. As a teen, Janis continued to write for leisure and was chosen to participate in a two-week journalism summer workshop for minority students on the campus of Buffalo State University, where she attended the following fall semester.

Throughout her career in mental health, Janis continued to hone her writing skills. While establishing her private practice, she joined HubPages writing site in 2012, where she continues to publish poetry and informational articles on various subjects such as relationships, loss, trauma, spirituality, wellness, and more recently, issues related to racial healing. She recently added Medium to her sites to post thoughts and poems.

Janis is also a member of the American Counseling Association and the Association for Spiritual, Ethical and Religious Values in Counseling. She is certified by the National Association of Certified Counselors and is also a member of the Facebook group Clinicians of Color in Private Practice.

For inquiries, interviews, or speaking engagements, contact the author at:
Book website: www.janislevans.com
Counseling Practice website: www.jlevanslpc.com
Twitter-X: @evans_janis
Instagram: @janislieevans